Autism, Play and Social Interaction

by the same author

Autism and Play
Jannik Beyer and Lone Gammeltoft
ISBN-13: 978 1 85302 845 8   ISBN-10: 1 85302 845 2

of related interest

Replays
Using Play to Enhance Emotional and Behavioural Development
for Children with Autism Spectrum Disorders
Karen Levine and Naomi Chedd
ISBN-13: 978 1 84310 832 0   ISBN-10: 1 84310 832 1

Playing, Laughing and Learning with Children on the Autism Spectrum
A Practical Resource of Play Ideas for Parents and Children
Julia Moor
ISBN-13: 978 1 84310 060 7   ISBN-10: 1 84310 060 6

Homespun Remedies
Strategies in the Home and Community for Children
with Autism Spectrum and Other Disorders
Dion E. Betts and Nancy J. Patrick
ISBN-13: 978 1 84310 813 9   ISBN-10: 1 84310 813 5

Communicating Partners
30 Years of Building Responsive Relationships with Late Talking Children
including Autism, Asperger's Syndrome (ASD), Down Syndrome,
and Typical Development
Developmental Guides for Professionals and Parents
James D. MacDonald
ISBN-13: 978 1 84310 758 3   ISBN-10: 1 84310 758 9

Autism, Play
and Social Interaction

Lone Gammeltoft and Marianne Sollok Nordenhof

Jessica Kingsley Publishers
London and Philadelphia

First published in 2007
by Jessica Kingsley Publishers
116 Pentonville Road
London N1 9JB, UK
and
400 Market Street, Suite 400
Philadelphia, PA 19106, USA

www.jkp.com

Library of Congress Cataloging in Publication Data
Gammeltoft, Lone, 1951-
  [Autisme, leg, og social udvikling. English]
  Autism, play, and social interaction / Lone Gammeltoft and Marianne
Sollok Nordenhof ; translated by Erik van Acker.
    p. ; cm.
  Includes bibliographical references and index.
  ISBN-13: 978-1-84310-520-6 (alk. paper)
  ISBN-10: 1-84310-520-9 (alk. paper)
  1. Autism in children. 2. Social interaction. 3. Social skills. 4. Play.
  I. Nordenhof, Marianne Sollok, 1958- . II. Title.
  [DNLM: 1. Autistic Disorder. 2. Child. 3. Interpersonal Relations.
  4. Play and Playthings.   WM 203.5 G193a 2006a]
  RJ506.A9A9844 2006
  618.92'85882—dc22

                                                        2006026313

British Library Cataloguing in Publication Data
A CIP catalogue record for this book is available from the British Library

ISBN-13: 978 1 84310 520 6
ISBN-10: 1 84310 520 9

Printed and bound by Amity Printing
in The People's Republic of China
APC-FT4774

Contents

Preface

This book arose from a desire we have had for a long time to pass on our experiences of how children with autism can improve their social skills by playing together in a group.

It was developed from the experiences described in *Autism and Play* by Jannik Beyer and Lone Gammeltoft (1998) and is based on the theoretical frame of reference described in that book.

This book is intended to be a source of ideas with practical examples of group games targeted at children with autism spectrum disorder (hereafter referred to as children with autism). The ideas can be used by both parents and professionals.

Our collaboration on play began in 1993 at Broendagerskolen, a school for children with autism and learning difficulties. At that time there was not much attention given to play as a way of working with children with autism, and the literature on the subject was very limited.

As playing is so vital in children's social development, we were surprised that playing had such a low priority in working with children with autism, so we decided to investigate whether playing could somehow make the social world more concrete and accessible for such children. That is what this book tries to illustrate.

We have taken inspiration from many different sources, not least from the TEACCH Program (Treatment and Education of Autistic and related Communication-handicapped CHildren), and of course the children, who are the best indication of whether we are creating the right atmosphere for them to enjoy play.

We wish to thank those children and parents who have inspired us.

Our warm thanks also to psychologist Maiken Toemming and speech therapist Anette Ly for constructive and critical comments on the manuscript.

Finally, special thanks to psychologist Jannik Beyer, who has been an inspirational sparring partner over the years.

Lone Gammeltoft and Marianne Sollok Nordenhof

Introduction

Peter Hansen (1868–1928) *Playing Children, Enghave Plads, Statens Museum for Kunst, Copenhagen (Photo: Hans Petersen)*

Playing occupies a large part of a child's life, and playing and childhood belong together. Through playing the child develops a variety of skills, not least in the social and emotional area. A child will always find a space in which to play, and playing is also recognized as children's very own occupation – their way of 'being' and expressing themselves.

The impulse to play is spontaneous for the children – they play because they just can't help it. Playing is an end in itself.

When children play together they intuitively prepare themselves to tune into a kind of common 'transmitter/receiver channel' with a high degree of mutual attention to each other. This means that very early on in life they practise listening: waiting for and reacting to each other's signals – all that is implied in social interaction. They learn basic social rules in a natural context; for instance that you have to take turns and that you cannot choose or win every time.

Through playing children build up close emotional relations, in which they both copy and test themselves against each other. Playing is an activity driven by pleasure and can involve joy, enthusiasm, absorption, excitement, anger and seriousness – whatever heightens the experience. All in all, playing must be considered fundamentally important to the development of the child.

Some children, for various reasons, do not have a natural approach to playing – and children with autism, among others, belong to this group. Children with autism find it difficult to interact socially with one another – and consequently they are often seen as children who can't learn to play with others. But if the play is organized by grown-ups on the children's terms, the children find a common platform where – through play – they can gain social experiences, which otherwise can be difficult for them to obtain.

When we talk about play, we are primarily concerned with the social aspect of it, focussing on the interaction between children without the intervention of grown-ups. The social world is difficult to explain. We only get to understand it by engaging with it. One way for children with autism to do this is for them to play with their peers, whether they are other children with autism or other learning difficulties or their brothers or sisters. The games described in this book can be enjoyed by and be of benefit to any child, and they are designed such that even if the children do not understand their purpose, that need not put them off playing.

The games that we describe all take place in a very organized setting, which gives the children the chance to see each other taking the initiative and relating to each other. The games are all based on actual and visual materials used in ordinary children's play. There are examples of how a play environment can be built up through careful organization and the use of visual cues, and how the togetherness of children at play can promote social awareness. The purpose is to create a forum for children where a joint agenda and a shared understanding of what they are doing together ensures a common focus of attention. Clearly setting out the agenda using visual cues helps the children understand what they are going to be doing together and can help them moderate their own impulses and ideas.

Clearly defined limits, both physical and abstract, help children with autism to concentrate on each other and in that way to respond appropriately in a social atmosphere.

As the social aspect is very difficult to clarify and visualize, the starting point for the shared experience must be a concrete and visual stimulus. At the outset we took part in the games with the children, but eventually we discovered that our presence was too obtrusive – we were interfering with the interaction between the children. From that time onwards we realized that we had to be invisible to provide space for the children to observe each other. We altered the parts so that we handed over the stage to the children and became 'stage managers', providing support through our work 'backstage'.

As the games are simple and visually clear, the children do not need any special instructions. Of course there are exceptions when the grown-up can either teach the games to the children one by one or participate in the group until the new game is known to everybody.

The games must be continuously adjusted and adapted to each individual child and group so that the children get the degree of visual support that they need.

It is a good idea to videotape the children playing, so that it is not only possible to see what succeeded and/or failed but also to find out what the children think is fun – which can be something completely different from what we imagined.

A playgroup can consist of two to six children. The children are chosen according to a variety of criteria: temperament, level of social development, personality and interests. For instance, it can be an advantage to put together a temperamental girl with calmer friends or a quiet, cautious boy with younger children.

A game session typically lasts from 15 to 60 minutes.

Educational approach
to playing

SOCIAL INTERACTION

For most people, navigating the social world is intuitive and entirely natural. We are well equipped to read and understand other people's intentions and feelings. We receive a lot of information just by looking at other people, and we instinctively try to create the best atmosphere for making social interactions succeed. How we do it is not easy to explain.

Children with autism do not seem to be equipped with the same innate social awareness. That is why we must lend them a hand by creating a framework for social interaction. Once we have we compensated for their social difficulties by creating meaningful limits in the phsysical space and through rules, the children can take part in social interaction without grown-ups being in control. The limits must support children in understanding what they are doing together and what they can expect from their interaction.

The following describes how you can create the ground rules for social interaction through the use of visual cues.

VISUALIZATION

The use of visual cues can make the presence of a grown-up unnecessary and improves the children's understanding and gives them independence.

By visualization we mean the use of objects or images as visual cues to explain a situation. Children with autism have difficulty transforming their impulses into appropriate action. They have difficulty creating method and order in what they do ('executive function') and their actions often seem to be random and out of context. They also have difficulty grasping the meaning of a situation ('central coherence'). For these reasons the children benefit considerably from structured education in which schedules, records, instructions and the like become visual, specific templates for the planning by which the rest of us navigate internally. Visualization is a support tool for a person with autism, like a white stick for the blind. Children with autism are often good at using their visual sense. By using visualization the children are able to function unaided in a range of contexts in which they would normally depend on the support of grown-ups.

Visualizing the limits of games condition the children for taking part in social interaction without grown-ups.

The advantages of using visualization in working with children with autism are that:

- images are concrete and non-transient, unlike, for instance, words, gestures and signs, so the information is clear and unambiguous

- it provides information in a form that many children can understand more easily than auditory information (i.e. spoken language) (Hodgdon 1995)

- it is possible to edit the information by extracting and illustrating both the order of events and the meaning of the situation.

Organizing games

Children with autism have great difficulty keeping their attention on a shared activity with others. They are often distracted by internal and external stimuli, or they become sidetracked by what we consider irrelevant details. They often have their own agenda and ideas of what the interaction should be about, but they never manage to communicate these ideas and intentions to each other. All of this makes it difficult for them to take part in a community.

The setting up of a common agenda therefore becomes a fundamental requirement for making interaction succeed for these children.

THE LIMITS OF THE GAME

In the following we describe how setting limits to the game helps the child to understand the common agenda.

Where will the game take place?

Children without special needs can play anywhere. They choose the physical space where the game is to take place and set it up together. They rarely have problems with a common focus and maintain the momentum of the game.

For children with autism it is necessary to set up, in advance, an environment where visual cues (physical limits) tell the children where the game is to take place. These limits can also help to minimize the risk of distraction by external stimuli.

A table with chairs is a good way of naturally limiting the area in which the game takes place (Figure 2.1). The chairs mark a place for every participant. The children can observe the area and each other and in this way they are better able to keep their attention on a common activity. The table forms the starting point of the interaction and is the base where information is given out and stored, so that everybody knows their place. Games that take place elsewhere can be delimited in different ways, using mats, carpets, bookcases or a taped area.

Figure 2.1 A table helps to limit the area in which the game takes place

What are we sharing?

An important condition for playing with other children is that you agree on *what* you are going to do together. For children without special needs it is easy to come up with a game that can be played by mutual agreement, because they can normally find something in common. Children with autism do not have extensive experience of playing with other children and therefore often bring along their own ideas on what interaction should be about.

A significant part of establishing a common agenda is that the game plan is given in advance and visualized so that the children know exactly *what* they will be doing together and for *how long* they will be together.

The simplest way in which to do this is to let the actual toys represent the game. In the beginning it may only be a single activity that the children do together. Over time you add other *simple* activities, which are kept in separate boxes. The boxes are put in a bookcase or the like, so that you can take them from left to right. When the last box has been used, the game is over (Figure 2.2).

Figure 2.2 Materials for each activity are kept in separate boxes

This is a system that, in any context, provides children with information on how many and which tasks they need to do. Interaction and playing demand much more from the children than just carrying out the tasks; hence it is important that they do not have to use all their energy on understanding and executing the activity itself, but can focus on doing it together with other children. The social aspect of playing a game is so challenging in itself that the content of the game must be simple and motivating.

A general game schedule with a clear visual indication of content and order is a simple way of outlining the activity. It is a good idea to have the contents consist of several small, short games rather than one larger, longer game. Shifting between the different games can be stimulating as long as the children are prepared for it.

The game schedule is numbered and each game is given a graphic symbol attached with Velcro (Figure 2.3). One of the children is in charge of the game session, which means that he or she is responsible for following the schedule correctly. As the children take turns at being the one in charge of the game session all participants have a chance to take responsibility in the course of the session (Figure 2.4). They often show great pride in taking on this role and get great satisfaction from following the system.

Figure 2.3 A numbered game schedule showing which games will be played and in what order

Graphic symbol number 1 is taken off the game schedule (Figure 2.5) and the corresponding toy put forward. When this game is finished, the toy is put aside and game number 2 begins. When the schedule is empty, the game session is finished. The last symbol, which is situated to the right of the schedule, is the timetable symbol. This means that

Figure 2.4 Order for taking responsibility for the game session

Figure 2.5 Taking off the graphic symbols

each child is able to check their daily timetable to see what the next activity is.

The game schedule is clear and easy to follow. All the children are prepared for exactly which game they are going to play and this gives them more energy to interact with each other.

As the children get to know the system, the child in charge can take responsibility for putting together the game schedule.

Who takes part in the game?

As children with autism have trouble taking the initiative to play with other children, it is essential that they know who takes part in the game. This information can be on their daily timetable. It is also important to clarify visually the order of the participants to make the game work as intended.

Giving a number to each child is a simple solution to this problem. The rule can be that the child in charge of the game always has the number 1 and that the other children get consecutive numbers and sit in this order. This way there are undisputed rules for which way to pass on a prop and whose turn it is – number 1 always starts. All this is

Figure 2.6 Numbers on the table show who sits where and the order of play

important so that children want, and understand how, to take part in the activity. By visualizing the order from the beginning you prevent disappointments and children going off to do their own thing.

The numbers should be ready on the table (Figure 2.6), so that when the children come to the table where the game is taking place, they find a number next to their picture corresponding with the number on the visual instruction. All the children are very quickly able to find their assigned position and stick the number onto their tops, so it is visible to everyone else. It gives the children great satisfaction to be able to read this information independently – comparable to the rest of us breathing a sigh of relief when we arrive at a big dinner party and find that there is a seating plan!

This kind of information can of course be presented in many ways, depending on the group of children you have. To make it easy for the children to handle the system of numbering themselves, the numbers can be printed on stick-on labels that are easy to attach to and remove from clothes.

It is a good idea for the game schedule to include taking off the numbers after the last game because, besides being a reminder, it also works as a logical indication that the game is over.

Whose turn is it?

An essential part of obeying the rules of a game is being able to take turns. This means that the children are able to take turns at carrying out an activity and at the same time feel that each participant's turn is part of the same activity.

Children with autism do not have taking turns incorporated into their rules of interaction and for that reason they have to learn it differently.

A cap can be a clear marker of who is taking the present turn – physically and visually. When the turn is done, the cap is passed on to the next in line according to the numbers.

When the principle is understood by all, the cap is used only on special occasions, for instance if the children need to slow down or when the game does not include any other way of indicating whose turn it is, such as a dice cup.

The 'taking turns' cap can remain an essential visualization of the cast in new and more sophisticated games, where it helps the children to stay focused on the person performing the task and manage the turn taking.

How should the materials be handled?

A problem shared by most children with autism, whatever their level of function, is having trouble organizing materials. If the organizing is not done in advance, important visual information can be messed up, materials can be mixed, and hence the game fails.

Organizing the materials is essential to the success of the interaction.

By making it clear *which* materials belong together, *how* they should be used and *where* each game starts and ends, you achieve a way of organizing materials or toys.

The toys are put in one spot: it can be a bookshelf, a desk or a trolley. The materials for each game are put into a box or are otherwise separated clearly (Figure 2.7).

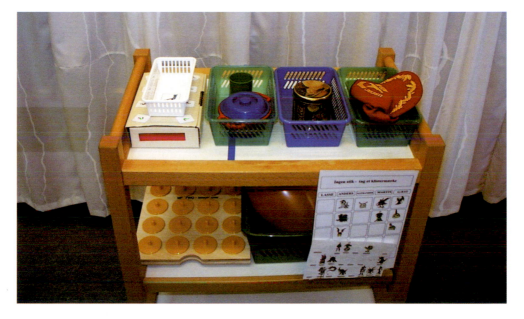

Figure 2.7 Careful organisation and separation of materials for different games facilitate play

In each game it may be necessary to show where the materials are to be placed. For instance, small boxes can indicate where to put tricks in a game of cards (Figure 2.8). It might seem like a small detail, but it is important to keep count of how many tricks each person has. Without the small boxes the tricks get mixed with the main pile or with the

Figure 2.8 Small boxes indicate where to put tricks in a game of cards

tricks of others. There is a high risk of the tricks falling on the floor and the time spent picking them up again spoils the flow of the game.

Besides, clear organization adds a certain joy to the game, which we may not share or quite understand, but which is very significant for children with autism – that things match and order exists.

Where does the game start and finish?

A clear indication of when a game starts and finishes is very important. A typical way of indicating start and finish is to begin with all the materials in one basket and put them into another basket as the game proceeds. When the first basket is empty and the materials are all in the second basket the game is finished.

If the materials for the game are not clearly separated and where you start and finish are not indicated, at some point the children will lose track of where they have got to. They may even start all over again with the materials that have already been used and hence lose interest.

In a game in which the children pull out cards from a basket, not only should the baskets be very different, but the final basket (or box) should have only a small slot through which to post the used cards – like a postbox. In this way the children never have any doubt about which basket to pick up the cards from (Figure 2.9).

Figure 2.9 To avoid confusion, make it clear from where the children are to pick up the cards and where to put them down when they have finished with them

A clear indication of start and finish is possible with basically all materials.

For instance, blowing bubbles can be a difficult, unorganized activity to share. The start will be clear only to the first participant, but what indicates when it is the time to pass on the dispenser? And when does the game finish? In addition, blowing bubbles is an activity in which much can go wrong – the dispenser might be dropped or knocked over, bringing the game to a premature end. But if everything is organized in one box, so you start by taking the 'blowing stick', dip it in the soapy water, blow the bubbles, put the stick back in the dispenser and pass on the box to the next in line, then the game is obvious and easy to play (Figure 2.10).

A small alarm clock or timer can be used as the finishing signal in games for which the materials themselves do not provide a built-in finish (Figure 2.11).

Figure 2.10 Making the game obvious and easy to play

Figure 2.11 Use an alarm clock or a timer to indicate the time limits on a game

Your careful organization can help the children play unassisted and motivate them.

The directions for use should be built into the material itself, that is, they should be so visually clear that further explanation is necessary only when introducing new games. If the children themselves cannot deduce the information from the material, the visualization is not sufficient. The sustainability of a game is measured by whether the children are immediately able to read what the game is all about. It is the duty of the grown-up to make the game as clear as possible.

The children will find that they can cope with the situation when it is clear:

- where the game takes place
- what each game is about
- who takes part in the game
- how the materials should be handled
- where the game starts and finishes.

The children now understand the common agenda and are ready to relate to each other.

INDIVIDUAL SYSTEMS OF SUPPORT

It is in itself a great challenge for children with autism to engage in social interaction.

Individual systems of support may be necessary as a supplement for some children to allow them to handle different situations to best effect without assistance.

Reminders

These are visual expressions of appropriate behaviour that the child must remember to abide by. A red line through a picture of what the child is not supposed to do, such as picking one's nose, is a precise and very simple way of providing information. These 'reminders' can be attached to the table in front of the child, which helps the child to remember the information (Figure 2.12).

Figure 2.12 Visual cues to prompt appropriate behaviour

Losing and winning

To many children it is difficult to lose – sometimes to the point of inconsolability. This also applies to children with autism. This may have to do with the fact that when you win you obtain something tangible – a trick in a game of cards or a prize. When you lose you get nothing.

Based on this understanding of losing and winning, as an intermediate stage, the loss can be made actual and visual if the children also get something when they lose, as a kind of consolation prize.

The example on page 27 shows a scorecard with the names of the children: if you don't get tricks in a game of cards you get a sticker instead (Figure 2.13).

In the game schedule that the children share – the one in which they can see which games are to happen– make it clear which games include 'lose and win'. Next to the symbol of the game in question put the symbol of the relevant scorecard. The children now know that they are to find the sheet with 'no trick – take a sticker' together with the other materials.

Figure 2.13 Consolation scorecard using stickers

Examples of games

The games in this book are primarily intended to increase children's attention to each other, on the assumption that when children are in a social situation that is free from any unnecessary 'noise' they have the opportunity of actually *recognizing* each other as active co-players.

Motivation is the principal element of playing – without motivation there is no commitment. Motivation comes partly from being able to play independently of adult intervention if the game has been carefully prepared and organised. Much also depends on the nature of the game. In our experience, most games can be motivating, no matter what level of function the children have, as long as they:

- are simple
- are of limited duration and do not go on for too long
- have a clear aim, preferably competition.

Many of the games are based on other well-known ones, which have been visually adapted to make it easier for the children to involve ordinary children (such as brothers and sisters).

The objective is that the children improve the quality of their interaction with each other. This is reflected in how much the children involve each other during the game.

In the following we describe some games that the children can play by themselves.

SIMPLE GAMES

Putting in

Description: For children who are at an early stage of development, interaction can be developed by letting the children take it in turns to do a playing activity involving exchange. By exchange we mean that the children share a toy by taking turns being the one to give and the one to receive. By using exchange, the transition from 'only me' to 'we are together' is emphasized.

We start with activities that the children enjoy and that they can all do unassisted, such as putting simple jigsaw puzzles together, putting blocks into a box, matching two identical pictures. These skills are not challenging to the child; the challenge comes from the social element of co-operation.

Procedure: Two children are seated in front of each other. The material consists of a basket with bricks and a container (Figure 3.1). The first child puts a brick into the container and pushes the basket across to the second child (Figure 3.2), who puts a new brick into the container and pushes the basket back to the first child, and so on. When all the bricks are put in the container the game is over. Most children at an early stage of development are able to put bricks into a container unassisted, i.e. the basic skill is present. The new demand is that the child must learn to push the basket across to the other child every time he or she has put a brick into the container, an action that the grown-up can (physically) assist the child in doing at first. In our experience, most children quickly learn the process of taking turns as a routine. However, be aware that in terms of development it is easier to push an object back and forth than it is to pass something over to each other.

Give and take

Procedure: Another form of exchange is in the game of give and take. One child gives and the other takes (or receives), after which they switch parts so that they take turns at being the giver and the receiver.

The organization is concrete and visually clear as one child has the board and the other child has the basket with the counters (Figure 3.3). This replaces the direct involvement of the grown-up and increases the children's mutual attention.

Figure 3.1 Exchange: The first child puts a brick in the box...

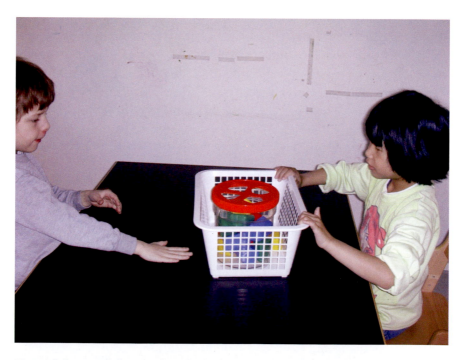

Figure 3.2 ...and then pushes the box over to the other child to have a go

Figure 3.3 Give and take: one child gives (in this case a piece of jigsaw) and the other receives

The children should be seated just within reach of each other, but not so close that the 'giver' can put the counter on the board him- or herself.

Purpose of both games: That the children see each other as necessary in order to succeed or to finish the activity through taking turns.

COMPLEX GAMES

Memory

Description: Memory is a very popular game, based on matching two identical pictures. Most children with autism are good at this and find it motivating.

The game is about the children taking turns to turn over two cards at a time, and if these cards are identical they get a trick. The point is to get the most tricks. The game has a clear ending, namely when all cards have been turned over and the tray is empty. Even so, there are several factors in the organization that need consideration before the children are able to play the game independently.

A limited number of pictures increases clarity. This keeps the game from slowing down and the players' attention from wandering.

A tray with panelled (raised) areas prevents the pieces from being mixed and at the same time shows whose turn it is, as the tray is easily passed on from child to child as a complete set, unlike when the pieces lie on the table.

Small numbered boxes – one for each participant – make it easier to keep your own tricks in order and the box is appealing in itself (Figure 3.4).

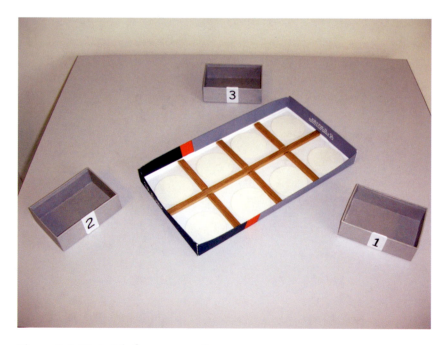

Figure 3.4 Materials for a game of memory

Procedure: Child 1 starts by turning over two cards – if they are identical, the child puts them in his or her trick box – and then passes on the tray to child 2 and so on. Each child is allowed to flip only two cards at a time, in order to cut the waiting time and at the same time increase the chance for everybody to take tricks. When the tray is empty the game is over.

Purpose: The children are motivated to keep a watch on each other and relate to one another through repeating the same actions as each other and expressing emotions such as joy and frustration, depending on the outcome of the game.

Sound-lotto

Description: Sound-lotto is a game that consists of an audio tape or CD with different sounds from daily life, illustrated by corresponding pictures. The principle is easy and is about matching sound and picture. The game is based on the sense of hearing. According to our experience it motivates the children to listen with great attention, which otherwise is very difficult for children with autism, as it can be hard to connect sounds to something concrete from daily life.

The organization is important and helps to make it easy for the children to handle the game themselves.

Procedure: Child 1 has the box intended for the pictures (which show whose turn it is) and turns on the tape recorder. The child listens, matches the sound to the corresponding picture by putting the picture into the box and then passes on the box to child 2, who listens and so on (Figure 3.5). When there are no more pictures on the table the game is over.

There are short breaks between sounds on the tape, so you don't have to turn the tape recorder on and off during the process. In this way the technical aspects do not interfere with the flow of the game.

Purpose: As in Memory, except that there is no winner in this game, which can be an advantage to some children.

Figure 3.5 Sound-lotto: the player listens and selects from the table the picture corresponding to a sound

Balloon game

Description: The balloon game requires the children to keep a balloon in the air without it ever touching the floor.

Procedure: The children sit or stand around a table. Child 1 can start by hitting the balloon across to one of the other children, who then hits it across to a third child, and so on (in random order) (Figure 3.6). The small alarm clock indicates when the game is over.

Depending on their level of ability a rule can be added that the children count how many times the balloon is hit without touching the floor (Figure 3.7).

Figure 3.6 Balloon game: the children must focus on each other…

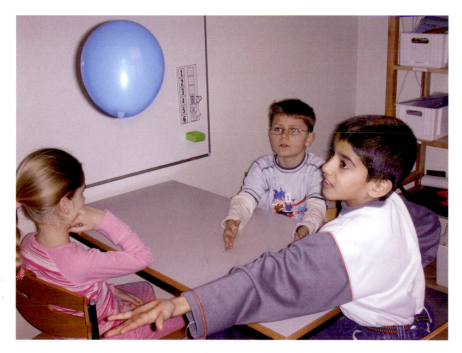

Figure 3.7 …to keep the balloon from touching the floor

Purpose: The children are motivated to co-operate and focus on each other in order to target their 'shots' as best they can. At the same time strong impulses in younger children can be restrained by making them remain seated. Older children are motivated by counting and breaking records. The game often arouses spontaneous joy and other emotional outbursts.

Hide and seek

Description: The children take turns to hide an object for one of the other children to find. There are two active participants in this game: the child who seeks the object and the child who hides it.

An important starting point is to make the object a small ticking clock in order to simplify the process of finding the object. The noise motivates the children to listen carefully in order to find the hiding place and at the same time this helps to keep the other children's attention on the person who is trying to find the clock.

It is important to limit the area in which the object can be hidden, so that the children know the ground covered by the game and are not distracted by irrelevant stimuli.

Procedure: The children sit in a circle or around a table. Child 1 leaves the room and the last child hides the clock, while the other children observe. Then everybody calls for child 1, who comes in and listens in order to find the hiding place. You can agree in advance that the other children may help by giving verbal support ('you're getting hot/cold') or by pointing, but they must all remain seated. The key factor is that the children keep their attention on each other. Then child 2 leaves the room, while child 1 hides the clock, and so on. The game is over when everybody has tried both hiding the object and finding it.

Purpose: Through playing, the children can achieve an understanding of hiding something from others, which can be a difficult concept for children with autism. Hiding something means understanding that you know something that others do not know and which you are not supposed to reveal. This can be difficult when you mainly understand the world from your own perspective, but it can normally be learned as a rule of the game.

At the same time the children are challenged to maintain attention on the two principal people: first the child who is to hide the clock and then the child who is to find it. This game can be a precursor for playing hide and seek with people, where you replace the clock with one of the children, who hides – and later on with all the children hiding from the one child who is supposed to find the others.

In this way you can simplify a relatively complicated game such as hide and seek by dividing it into several elements that are learned step by step.

Shopkeeping

Description: Shopkeeping is a simple game that most children have played for generations. This version is based on exchanging pictures; it was inspired by PECS (Picture Exchange Communication System), which allows children who are unable to communicate verbally to use pictures as a communication system. The game is also popular among children who can talk and would not otherwise use PECS, because the system is based on the principle of *being given* something.

Procedure: The children take turns being 'shopkeeper' (wearing the turn-taking cap). The shopkeeper stands behind a counter with different kinds of goods. The pictures of the goods are hung on a board, kept apart from the counter (Figure 3.8). The other children can

Figure 3.8 Shopkeeping: pictures of the goods are attached to a wall or board

choose whatever they want by taking a corresponding picture; they give it to the shopkeeper, who will then give each child the requested goods (Figure 3.9). Each child puts the used picture back on the board when he or she has finished 'using' or eating the goods. An alarm clock indicates when the shopkeeper must switch parts, which means that he or she passes on the cap to child 2, and so on. The game is over when all the children have been the shopkeeper.

Figure 3.9 The shoppers hand over the pictures to the shopkeeper in exchange for the goods

Purpose: The children play with the exchange routine through dialogue: approaching a receiver (the shopkeeper) directly, they deliver a message (a picture) in order to receive an answer (the requested object).

Game of dice

Description: The children sit around a table on which there is a cup with a dice, which has colours instead of numbers, and a bowl containing a limited number of sweets in different colours.

Procedure: Child 1 throws the dice and takes one sweet in whatever colour the dice shows (Figure 3.10). The cup is passed on to child 2, who throws, and so on. The game is over when there are no more sweets left in the bowl. This is very simple and at the same time motivating.

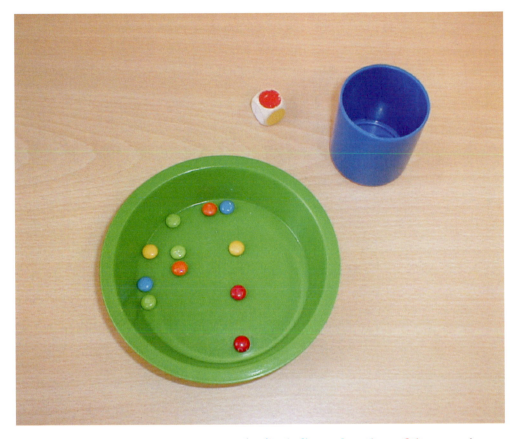

Figure 3.10 Game of dice: the colour on the dice indicates the colour of the sweet that can be taken

Comment: There are some 'jokers' in the game. What happens if a child throws a green and there are no green sweets left? You get nothing. The basis of the game is that the rules have to be followed and in this case it is the dice that decides.

Purpose: Through this simple game of dice the children learn that the outcome is not always in your favour when you are with others, but fortunately you have another turn in a little while and perhaps you will be luckier then. The children are thus encouraged to keep an eye on each other to ensure that the rules are followed.

Meanwhile the lucky children can gloat over their luck – all in all, emotional expressions that provide important social experiences about yourself and others.

See also Never mind, as on page 53.

Spin the bottle

Description: Spin the bottle is a familiar game, in which the children sit with a bottle placed in the middle. The person whose turn it is spins the bottle. When the bottle stops the person at whom the bottleneck points performs an action decided by the person who spun the bottle (Figure 3.11).

Figure 3.11 Spin the bottle: the bottleneck points out who is to mime next

To make it easier for the children to play the game, what the person pointed out by the bottleneck should do may be specified in advance. The visualization consists of different cards with a picture and/or text describing simple activities (clapping, waving, jumping, and so on) organized in some sort of a card holder, so that they can easily be passed back and forth between the participants.

Procedure: The children sit on the floor or around a table. Child 1 spins the bottle and the child pointed out by the bottleneck draws a card and does whatever the card indicates. Then the card is put into a box through a slit in the lid, so that the card disappears. Then this child spins the bottle, and so on. When there are no more cards in the holder the game is over.

If the bottle is too difficult to handle the game can be simplified by the children taking turns to draw cards.

Purpose: The children learn that not everyone necessarily gets the same number of turns because the order in this game is random (you can't predict where the bottleneck will point). Besides it can be difficult to agree on who is being pointed at when the bottle is pointing at the space between two children. These issues can challenge the children to try to find a solution themselves, which is a good opportunity for them to practise reaching an agreement.

Pass the parcel

Description: This game is a popular parlour game in which the contestants throw a dice in a limited period of time in order to win the one parcel that is in the game. The game requires one toy wrapped in paper, a dice (preferably with only three numbers in order to speed up play) and a small alarm clock. The principle of the game is simple, it is visually clear and there is a clear indication of when the game starts and ends.

Procedure: The children sit around a table or in a circle on the floor. Child 1 throws the dice and then passes on the cup to child 2, and so on, and whoever gets the number 3 on the dice can take the parcel (but not open it) and put it in front of him or her. The children continue throwing the dice and every time one of them gets the number 3 he or she can take the parcel. Whoever has the parcel in front of him or her when the alarm clock rings can open the parcel and the contents are shared or used in turns. It is not something that the winner gets to keep to him- or herself.

The timeframe can be adjusted according to how many children are taking part in the game. The optimal number of participants is four to five children.

Purpose: In this game there is a good 'flow'; the clock helps to speed it up and the children are motivated to keep an eye on each other. The element of competition stimulates the children to express, and to notice in themselves and in the others, spontaneous emotions such as excitement, expectation, joy, frustration – all of which reflect a committed interaction.

Mouse

Description: Mouse involves putting treats such as raisin, popcorn or sweets on a colourful patterned plate. The child whose turn it is eats the treats one by one until he or she takes the 'mouse', which the other children decided on beforehand (Figure 3.12). The colours and pattern on the plate help the children select and remember the 'mouse'. You could also use a plain plate and different coloured sweets, but it works best with only one of each colour.

Procedure: The children sit around a table. Child 1 leaves the room (or closes his or her eyes), while the other children must agree on one of the treats to be the 'mouse'. Then child 1 comes back to the table and starts eating one treat at a time, while he or she keeps an eye on the other children's reaction. When the child picks up the 'mouse' the other children shout 'MOUSE' and this treat must not be eaten. The point is of course to get as many treats as possible. Then child 2 leaves the room and so on, until all of the children have had their turn.

Comment: Depending on the group of children involved, this game may require some adjustments for the children themselves to be able to control it.

Agreeing on selecting a 'mouse' at first is challenging for the children; hence the other rules are simplified as much as possible in order to get the interaction to function.

Giving the children numbers may be essential for the children themselves to handle the order in which they are to take turns.

Figure 3.12 Mouse: the player can take treats from the plate until he or she picks the 'mouse'

The 'taking-turns' cap can be used as a further visualization of whose turn it is, in order to highlight the current player to the other children and so focus their attention on him or her.

Before you start the game you can read out some rules for playing Mouse to the children. For example:

When we play Mouse I must remember:

- to point at the treat that we have agreed to be the 'mouse' (and not say it out loud)
- that whoever has the 'taking-turns' cap must eat only one treat at a time until the others call out 'MOUSE'
- that, when it is my turn, I do not know which treat the others have chosen to be 'mouse'

- that I do not know how many treats I will get
- that sometimes I will get lots and sometimes I may get none, but that is OK
- if I do not get any treats, I can try again next time we play Mouse.

Purpose: In this game you can be unlucky and get nothing! Again we have a game based on maintaining attention on each other. But there are other elements in the game, for instance being able to change perspective and strategy. Through playing the children get an understanding of keeping the 'mouse' secret from the child in question, which means that the other children have a different perspective on the game from their playmate. In addition it becomes clearly necessary to select a new treat to be the 'mouse' every time (to change strategy) in order to 'fool' the playmate.

Guessing game

Description: The guessing game is about the children taking turns to mime an activity or an emotion; the other children then have to guess what is being mimed.

Procedure: The children sit around a table. Child 1 picks a card and mimes whatever the words or picture on the card indicate (without showing the card to the others!) and the other children try to guess what the mime signifies. Then the card is put in a 'completed' box and the card holder is passed on to child 2 and so on (Figure 3.13). The game is over when there are no more cards left.

Comment: It is a good idea to start with simple actions – for instance everyday routines. It is easier for both the miming child and the other children to relate to an activity such as combing your hair, drinking, brushing your teeth, dancing. When the children have become familiar with the idea of the game, it can be extended to miming more complex actions and emotions.

Purpose: The object of this game is to direct the children's attention to reading other people's body language and imitations (which can be

Figure 3.13 Materials for the Guessing game

difficult for children with autism) in a simple miming game. The children are encouraged to keep their attention on the person doing the mime. In addition the children learn that they can put into action visual information from a card, without first showing the card to the others.

Eenie, meenie

Description: Children's rhymes are a way in which children can play with the language in a rhythmical way, which most ordinary children love, especially because there is often a social element in saying these rhymes together. To many children with autism rhymes do not appeal in the same way. In order to get the children to see the point of saying these rhymes and at the same time make it a coherent social interaction, you can use a box with small edible treats.

Figure 3.14 Eenie, meenie…

Figure 3.15 …minie, moe

Figure 3.16 Whoever gets to say 'toe' can open the box and take a treat

Procedure: The children sit in numerical order on the floor or around a table. They say the rhyme as the box is being passed from child to child (in numerical order): Eenie (1) – meenie (2) – minie (3) – moe (4) – catch (1) – a tiger (2) – by the (3) – toe (4). The child who gets the box on 'toe' can open the box and take a treat (Figures 3.14 to 3.16). The game is repeated until the box is empty (adjust the number of treats to the number of children).

Who gets the 'toe' depends on the number of children. When two children are together they will get the 'toe' every second time. When three children are together the rule is that whoever got the 'toe' shall begin the next round, and so on. That way everybody gets the 'toe'. This can be visualized for the children on a plan.

Purpose: This is a game that focuses on taking turns and starting/stopping. The passing on of the box visualizes the rhyme by basing it on action in a tangible and motivating way. Some children with autism are good at repeating and remembering linguistic expressions; thus they are given an insight into social experience by saying the rhyme together with other children. At least one of the children must know the rhyme.

Star game

Description: The star game is homemade and is based on principles known from other board games. It consists of a board with differently coloured areas, correspondingly coloured cards with a picture or some text, counters, a dice and sweets (Figure 3.17).

The cards and the sweets are arranged in a box with compartments. This version of the game requires that at least one of the participants is able to read.

The board is divided into differently coloured areas with a 'Start' and 'Finish'. The cards are divided into five different categories:

- factual questions such as 'What is the capital of England?'
- personal questions such as 'Where did you spend your summer holiday?'
- riddles
- jokes
- treats.

Figure 3.17 Materials for the Star game

Each category has its own colour, which corresponds with an area on the board. In addition there are some white areas; landing here means that the player has to miss a turn. On some of the areas there is a star, which allows the player to move to the next star.

Procedure: The children sit around a table with the board in the middle. Every child selects a counter (or is given a numbered piece) and puts it on 'Start'. Child 1 controls the box with the cards and treats, and also reads out the questions throughout the game. (This task can be given to another child if child 1 cannot read.) Child 1 throws the dice and moves his or her counter according to the number on the dice. Depending on which colour the counter lands on, the child gets a question from the corresponding category or wins a treat. Whichever child is the first to reach 'Finish' is the winner and the game is over.

Purpose: The children learn to use simple topics of conversation when interacting with each other. Children with autism are definitely not used to small talk. This means that they often do not know very much about each other, for instance where they live or whether they have any brothers or sisters. They may not even know that they can ask one another in order to get information. All in all they are not used to exchanging factual knowledge with each other, making jokes and telling riddles. The game is a formalized exercise for the children in taking turns at this kind of exchange.

GAMES WITH SOCIAL RULES

The following are some examples of how children with autism can learn the rules of social interaction through play, when those rules are expressed in terms of a game.

Social rules are necessary in order to make society function. As children acquire more social experiences, the need for rules to govern their interactions increases. Being able to follow such rules means understanding that it is the rules that decide in any given situation and not their own needs.

This means that the child must learn to accept that a situation does not always benefit him or her. This is not easy for children, who cannot help but see the world from their own perspective, but it is essential for coping in the social world. How then do we teach the children this? We do it by putting the children in situations where they, so to speak, absorb the rules according to the principle of 'learning by doing'. So, instead of protecting the children from situations of conflict, we make the conflict into an experience that offers the children possible actions. Only in this way can we prepare the children for handling the situations themselves in future – a sort of early conflict resolution.

The advantage of children learning through playing is that we set up situations in which the children are mentally relaxed and not really subject to social pressure. Social rules cannot be taught in social relations in which the child is in the middle of a crisis.

The inspiration for using different graphic symbols as tools is drawn from Picture Exchange Communication System (PECS).

Home

If we think back to our own childhood, we realize that we learned many social rules through playing with other children. This happened without our knowledge; the rules were absorbed subconsciously.

Among such rules is, for instance, the concept of 'home'. Most of us probably recall shouting 'HOME', just before we were caught – the feeling of being able to choose a break or a *haven* when we were most under pressure.

Grown-ups can also benefit greatly form the concept of 'home', albeit a mental refuge, to switch off for a while to gather their throughts before rejoining the real world.

Children with autism tend to be poor at this mental housekeeping. They receive impressions unsorted and hence they are often overwhelmed by stimuli from their surroundings. The consequence can be that the children switch off or feel unwell and have difficulty maintaining concentration.

Hence children with autism are dependent on *us* to sort impressions and stimuli for them. Structured teaching, based on visualizing everyday activities, demonstrates that, when this sorting succeeds, the children relax, focus on the task at hand and hence are better able to achieve their potential.

But how do you sort stimuli in the social arena? In social relations, which are so demanding for a child with autism to participate in, children need to learn how to take time out without physically leaving.

Experience shows that if we translate and clarify the rules of the social world in the children's terms, they are actually able to learn and make use of these rules.

Description/purpose: To give the children an understanding of what 'home' means, the grown-ups must stage situations that go slightly beyond the children's boundaries – situations that cause the children to need to step aside. Teasing is an example of a situation which is often difficult to handle, so it can help to teach the children to tease each other in a way that is controllable. That is to offer the children an actual (emotional) experience of being able to tease somebody in an acceptable and clearly defined way, without the child or the relationship falling apart.

To some children a 'social script' can be a useful starting point for a representation of 'home' (Figure 3.18).

Figure 3.18 A 'social script' is a useful starting point for a representation of 'home'

This way the children gain an understanding, through play, of the concept 'home'.

Procedure: Two or three children sit at a table and the materials and rules of the game are introduced to the children (Figure 3.19).

- Child 1 draws a card from a holder (containing eight to ten different cards).

- The child does to the other children whatever is shown on the card; for instance, tickle with a feather, stick his or her tongue out, use provocative words.

- When one of the children feels put under pressure, he or she can put on the red cap and say 'HOME', and step out of the game (Figure 3.20).

- When the child takes off the cap he or she re-enters the game.

- Now child 2 draws a card, and so on.

- When the card holder is empty the game is over.

Figure 3.19 Materials for the Home game

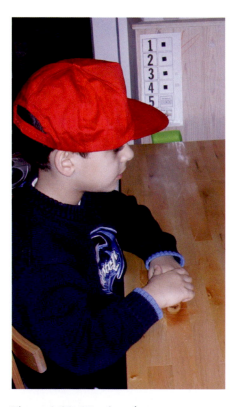

**Figure 3.20 Wearing the cap means
being 'home' – and not
participating in the game**

This way, through playing, the children quickly get an early understanding of the concept of 'home' in a simple and fun way.

Subsequently the grown-ups must be sure to integrate the concept in the children's everyday lives by making the cap available to the children wherever they go, inside as well as outside the home.

Over time the 'home cap' can be replaced by a graphic symbol.

Exchanging toys

Description: When children with autism learn to play together they need some literal 'social tools' to help them handle being together.

Some children tend to become so absorbed in a particular toy that they show no real interest in togetherness. Others find it difficult to approach each other in an appropriate way.

So, it is the task of the grown-ups partly to make it meaningful for the children to involve each other in the game and partly to provide them with clear rules for how this can be done.

Procedure: The children can learn to interact through playing with the help of a 'swap card'. To begin with, the rules are made as simple as possible, in order to make the exchanging routine become the main purpose. Start with just two children together, each with a motivating toy. The 'swap card' is put on the table between them, fastened with Velcro.

Most children will quickly learn to use the 'swap card' (Figure 3.21), which means taking the card, giving it to the playmate and saying: 'Shall we swap?'. The motivation is to try out the toys: first one's own and then the playmate's (Figure 3.22). This gives rise to the need for exchange.

Over time you can add more toys. Give each child a basket with different but complementary toys (toy figures, doll's house furniture, and so on). The point is the toys are different so the children are motivated to negotiate with each other.

When the children have learned the exchange rule as a routine, introduce the 'swap card' in everyday situations.

Purpose: Experience has shown that most children very quickly learn that the 'swap card' has a direct impact on the playmate, which otherwise can be hard to obtain without conflict. The card provides both sides with an opportunity to respond, thereby increasing their attention towards each other – so instead of just grabbing the toy you want

Figure 3.21 'Shall we swap?'

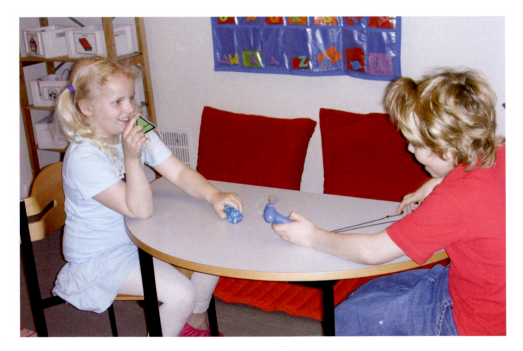

Figure 3.22 Exchanging toys

(and the game falling apart) the card sets the stage for negotiation, which means dialogue, before the desired action is executed (and the game goes on).

Shall we play with…? YES/NO

Description: Many children with autism find it difficult to initiate moves to play with other children. And if they have tried it is often linked to negative experiences. However, if the children have a formalized tool to ask each other 'Shall we play?' and at the same time very precisely indicate what they should play, the children themselves have a basis for approaching each other without being misunderstood.

Procedure: Two children sit in front of each other at a table. Pictures of possible toys are fastened with Velcro on a wall or board nearby (Figure 3.23).

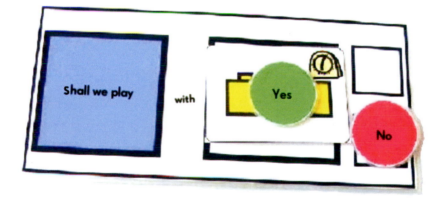

Figure 3.23 Materials for Shall we play with…? YES/NO

Child 1 chooses one of the pictures from the board and sticks it on to a strip of Velcro, hands it over to the playmate and asks (if he or she is able to use spoken language): 'Shall we play with building bricks?' The playmate replies by putting the YES or NO symbol on top of the picture. If the answer is YES, child 1 picks up the toy, which is nearby, and the children play until the game reaches its own conclusion or an alarm clock sounds. The children take turns asking and answering each other. If the answer is NO the child who asked must play with the toy alone or come up with another suggestion.

Purpose: In this game the children have a tool that helps them approach and await each other's reply in a formalized way – the substance of a dialogue.

The children learn that it is OK to disagree and that you can solve it by asking again.

Waiting game

When you *wait for something* it means that you cannot expect to have all your desires satisfied at once. In other words, waiting for something means postponing your desires. This is difficult for most people – think of a tailback during rush hour. All young children must learn to wait and all parents know that it does not happen without difficulty.

For children with poor imagination, an understanding of the concept is essential in order to be able to relate to it. They need to learn that waiting for something means *postponement* and not *never*.

In order to prepare the children in the best possible way to handle a postponement of their desires, a visualization of the concept can be a great help.

Description: The waiting game uses the authorized PECS-symbol for 'wait' (fastened with Velcro to the middle of the table) and graphic symbols of different options (fastened to a strip). The corresponding actual objects are placed a short distance from the table (Figure 3.24).

Procedure: Child 1, wearing the cap, asks child 2 'What would you like?' and at the same time hands over the strip with the graphic symbols. Child 2 chooses one of the pictures and hands it back to child 1, who says 'wait' and gives child 2 the waiting card. Child 1 leaves the table and picks up the requested object, returns to the table, takes the waiting card and hands the object to child 2. When the object has been used or eaten child 1 hands over the cap to child 2, who asks child 3 and so on, until all the children have tried both roles.

Figure 3.24 Materials for the Waiting game

Purpose: This way the children grasp the concept in a motivating and accessible way through play.

The graphic symbol for 'wait' can easily be used in relevant situations in the children's everyday lives.

Never mind

We got the idea of the Never mind game from a boy in Broendagerskolen who used the expression 'never mind' to defuse conflict situations, which are inevitable in day-to-day social interactions.

To say 'never mind' is analogous to the concept 'home'. It involves a more mental acceptance of the fact that social rules are not always to your advantage but that your world does not fall apart because of it.

Description: A simple game of dice with coloured dice and sweets (as described in Game of dice on page 38) is an ideal way to introduce the concept. The 'never mind' card is put in the middle of the table with

Figure 3.25 Whenever a child makes a throw of the dice that does not result in a sweet, he or she can take the 'Never mind' card

Figure 3.26 Never mind!

Velcro (Figure 3.25). Whenever a child makes a throw that does not result in a sweet, he or she can take the card and say 'never mind' (Figure 3.26).

Purpose: Children learn to handle the feeling that everything is not always to your advantage when you play by the rules.

Experience shows that when children are given the opportunity to be specific about this feeling – by taking the card and saying 'never mind' out loud – the situation is put into perspective. In this way the child in crisis reduces his or her impulses to, for instance, hit or destroy something or have a tantrum, and in many cases they find it easier to accept the situation.

Simply stated, the 'never mind' card is a visualization of the inner thought processes that the rest of us use in order to handle or adapt to disadvantageous situations.

Epilogue

To many people the joy and the meaning of social life is in togetherness itself — sharing experiences, thoughts, reflections, joys and sorrows.

To people with autism social life is often more of an obstacle, which does not make sense until it is translated into tangible and manageable values.

But to translate something that is based on intuition and feeling is, of course, only partly possible.

However, we are convinced that children with autism can engage in the social world through play, but this does not alter the fact that they will find it hard work. Social interaction is a challenging area for children with autism, and in the kind of play that we have described we are dealing with small steps in a very simplified translation.

But we see that the children have an increasing need to repeat the positive social experiences that occur whenever the settings make it possible for them to start playing unaided. And we see them spontaneously offering each other emotional responses during the games when they understand the premise of togetherness.

And *that* is a huge step towards what we consider a human right: to be able to share and exchange experiences on your own terms.

The games can easily be transferred to the home setting. We have known parents who have gathered the accessories for some of the games in a suitcase, which they take along to social gatherings with family or friends. In this way their child can initiate play with the other children there.

To create suitable limits for playing involves a real respect for these children's perceptions, so that we do not necessarily force our way of togetherness on to them but all the time are aware of what they find motivating, meaningful and fun. The children are the main characters and the grown-ups are backstage when it comes to the testing and adjustment required to develop the games.

Through this book we hope to have inspired others who work with children with autism to increase the opportunities for them to play together.

Bibliography

Baron-Cohen, S. (1987) 'Autism and symbolic play.' *British Journal of Developmental Psychology 5*, 139–149.

Beyer, J. and Gammeltoft, L. (2000) *Autism and Play*. London: Jessica Kingsley Publishers.

Broström, S. (1997) 'Children's play: Tools and symbols in frame play.' *Early Years 17*, 2, 16–21.

Elkonin, D. (1989) *The Psychology of Play*. USSR: Sputnik.

Frith, U. (1989) *Autism – Explaining the Enigma*. Oxford: Basil Blackwell Ltd.

Frost, L. and Bondy, A. (2002) *The Picture Exchange Communication System, Training Manual*. Newark: Pyramid Educational Products Inc.

Gray, C.A. (1995) 'Teaching Children with Autism to "Read" Social Situations'. In K.A.Quill (ed.) *Teaching Children with Autism: Strategies to Enhance Communication and Socialization*. Albany, NY: Delmar.

Happé, F. (1994) *Autism: An Introduciton to Psychological Theory*. London: UCL Press Limited.

Harris, P.L. (1989) *Children and Emotion*. Oxford: Basil Blackwell Ltd.

Hodgdon, L.A. (1995) *Visual Strategies for Improving Communication*. Michigan: Quirk Roberts Publishing.

Howlin, P. and Jordon, R (eds) (2003) 'Autism' *The International Journal of Research and Practice 7*, 4, Special Issue on Play.

Lord, C., Rutter, M. and Di Lavore, P. (2000) 'The Autism Diagnostic Observation Schedule – Generic: A Standard Measure of Social and Communication Deficits Associated with the Spectrum of Autism.' *Journal of Autism and Developmental Disorders 30*, 3.

Mesibov, G. and Shea, V. (1994) *The Culture of Autism: From Theoretical Understanding to Educational Practice*. New York: Plenum Press.

Nelson, K. and Seidman, S. (1984) 'Playing with Scripts.' In Inge Bretherton (ed.) *Symbolic Play*. New York:Academic Press.

Ozonoff, S., Pennington, B.F. and Rogers, S.J. (1991) 'Executive function deficits in highfunctioning autistic children: relationship to theory of mind.' *Journal of Child Psychology and Psychiatry 32*, 1081–1106.

Peeters, T. (1997) *Autism: From Theoretical Understanding to Educational Intervention.* London: Whurr.

Schopler, E. and Mesibov, G. (eds) (1995) *Learning and Cognition in Autism.* New York: Plenum Press.

Stern, D. (1985) *The Interpersonal World of the Infant.* New York: Plenum Press.

Trillingsgaard, A. (1999) 'The script model in relation to autism.' *European Child and Adolescent Psychiatry 8*, 45–49.

Wolfberg, P. (1995) 'Enhancing Children's Play.' In K.A. Quill (ed.) *Teaching Children with Autism: Strategies to Enhance Communication and Socialization.* Albany, NY: Delmar.

Index